Higher

GCSE Spanish for OCR

Exam Skills Workbook

Vincent Everett

OCR
RECOGNISING ACHIEVEMENT

OXFORD
UNIVERSITY PRESS

Official Publisher Partnership

OxBox

Contents

Contents of CD-ROM

Audio tracks
- Audio tracks from Pronunciation section
- Audio tracks from Listening practice section

Answers
- Answers to Listening practice section
- Answers to Vocabulary in practice section
- Answers to Worksheets section

Preparing for your GCSE

How to get an A*

1 Take control of your own grade

Find out what you need to do for a top mark, then set yourself targets to make sure you get there.
- If you think you've not really learnt something well enough, then make sure you spend some time working on it.
- Explore the useful sections of the  Students' Book and use them to surprise your teacher.
- This exam guide will help you know what to do to if you really want to do well.
- Practise exam questions to become familiar with the types of questions and content.

2 Know your vocabulary

Make sure your vocabulary grows. It is like rolling a snowball. The more vocabulary you already know, the easier it is for more and more new words to stick.
- Crack the Spanish spelling/pronunciation system. Then you will pick up new words quickly and accurately.
- Don't assume that intelligence will get you through the exam. If other people have learnt more words than you, they can get a better mark.
- Enjoy Spanish words. Pick out words that are nice to say. Practise saying tricky words and long words. Learn words that no-one else knows!
- Learn the exam board's defined content vocabulary which they publish in the syllabus.

3 Know your grammar

Think of grammar as a tool for expressing yourself.
- Have a core of grammar that you use for all topics: opinions, reasons, connecting words. Make sure you can give examples in the past and future and talk about other people, not just yourself.
- Think of grammar positively, as a tool for expressing yourself. Build up a range of structures to make you look good, and make sure you use them.
- Don't ignore the other side of grammar: check carefully for accuracy.
- Remember, everything you learn will become part of your Spanish.

4 Fall in love with Spanish
- Watch Spanish films on DVD, or listen to songs in Spanish.
- Explore Spanish culture on the internet and in magazines.
- Set the language on your video games console or phone to Spanish.
- Try sending Spanish texts and emails to your friends.

Come over on the dark side.

5 Show what you know
- Draw up a revision timetable and make sure you cover everything you need.
- Find out what you need to show in each exam (see Listening, Speaking, Reading and Writing sections, pages 4–22, this book), and make sure you can do it.

Preparing for the listening exam

1 Learn to listen
- Make sure you are confident with the Spanish sound/spelling system (see Pronunciation overview, pages 8–9, this book). You must be able to turn the sounds on the recording into a word in your head. Notice how words are joined together in spoken Spanish..
- Practise dictation with a friend or record yourself. Try to write down accurately what is being said in Spanish.
- Listening while reading the script at the same time helps you learn to keep track in longer listenings.
- Listen to Spanish films or music to get your ear tuned into Spanish.

2 Before listening
- Use any clues in the title, introduction or illustrations to help you focus on what you are going to hear.
- Use the questions to help predict the words and information to pick out.
- Think about possible choices and confusions: present/past/future, different people, numbers, changes of mind ...

3 While listening
- On the first listening, let your ears do the work. Focus on overall understanding. If you try to start answering the questions, you may miss important information.
- On the second listening, focus on detail.
- Watch out for negatives, time references, people who change their mind, connecting words that signal contrasts, and confusing situations involving more than one person.

4 After listening
- Use your brain to make sense of what you heard.
- Use your knowledge of the language and the country to make sensible guesses to any questions you aren't sure about.

Preparing for the speaking controlled assessment

1 A confident approach: be in control
- In the speaking tasks you can be confident that there will only be Spanish you know, because you are the one in charge of speaking the Spanish.
- Make sure you equip yourself for the task. You need to be good at giving opinions, points of view and talking about past and future. You need to be prepared to take the initiative and develop your answers.

2 Learn to speak
- Get used to speaking Spanish with a partner and record yourself to check your pronunciation, pace and intonation.
- Make sure you can understand questions and ask some of your own.
- Build up a core of Spanish that is useful for a range of topics.
- Build up routines that keep you talking: opinion → reason → example. If you mention someone, make them say something. Take yourself through the process of deciding: I was going to... but my dad said... so I decided to...
- Use connecting words to link and extend your answers. Use dice to keep talking: 1 and, 2 but, 3 because, 4 for example, 5 so, 6 especially if.
- Think of starting some questions with "if". It gives you two goes at the answer: if I go with my friends, then I like to... but if I have to go with my family, then...
- Get used to making the most out of each idea before you move on. Give opinions. Talk about who, where and when. Give examples in past and future.
- Have a clear idea of the Spanish in your range, and build up answers showing off what you can do.
- Learning the Spanish is only half the picture. You need to get good at thinking up what to say. Practise telling someone else what to say. You say it in English; they say it in Spanish. You'll find the hardest part is making up the ideas!

3 Preparing the task
- You will have time to prepare the Speaking assessment task. It may be a task that involves other students, but only one of you will be being assessed.
- You can discuss the task and how to approach it with your teacher, but they cannot help you with the Spanish.
- Use all your reference materials to prepare the task.
- Make prompt cards with words, pictures, etc. to help you carry out the task. You are allowed to take a speaking notes form into assessment with you, containing five bullet points with no more than eight words per bullet point.
- Have a check list in your head of the structures you want to show off.
  For example, bring your answers to life with direct speech: "He said...", "I said..."

4 Performing the task
- Listen carefully to the questions.
- Ask (in Spanish) if you want a question repeated. It is normal for your brain to need time to get going.
- Watch out for unexpected questions.
- If you can't remember what you were going to say, then think quickly of something else you can say.
- Use your connecting words to keep going until you are asked another question.
- Build answers out of the Spanish you want to show off.
- The task will be filmed or recorded and sent off to be marked.

Mr Smith. The examiners want to know why they can hear dice rolling at the end of each sentence.

Preparing for the reading exam

1 Learning to read Spanish
   - Even at Higher level, the easiest way to get more questions right is to learn more words.
   - Make sure you are confident with the Spanish sound/spelling system (see Pronunication overview, pages 8–9, this book). You must be able to turn the words on the page into sounds in your head.

2 Before reading
   - Read the instructions and make sure you know what you are meant to be reading.
   - If the text is on one page and the questions on the next, don't get caught out by only looking at one page!
   - Reading the questions first gives you clues to the content and tells you what to look for.
   - Often the answers will appear in the same order as the questions.
   - Watch out: some tasks ask you to hunt for the answer in several short passages. For example "Find the person who..." (🌏 see Reading section, Students' Book, pages 171–190).

They kept asking who did it, so I just put 'Yo no' for all those questions.

3 When reading
   - As well as using the questions to hunt for answers, read the text and get an overall understanding.
   - Watch out for details that seem to be hiding: the date at the top of the letter, the person's name at the end.
   - Use the words you do know to make sense of what it says and to work out the meaning of unfamiliar words.
   - If you have to answer in English, keep your answer close to what it actually says. This will show you understood the Spanish.
   - If you have to draw conclusions from what you read, make sure you find specific parts of the text that help come to an answer. Don't just give a vague response.
   - Put a sensible answer to all the questions, even if you are unsure of the right answer (🌏 see Reading section, Students' Book, pages 171–190).

Preparing for the written controlled assessment

1 Aiming for an A*

- You need to explain ideas, opinions and points of view. You will need to show off a variety of vocabulary and structures such as verb tenses. Each piece of writing will focus on a different format or purpose.
- You will be able to use your reference materials to prepare for the task, so make sure they are organised.
- Build up your own personal range of structures to narrate, explain and to bring your writing to life.

2 Preparing the task

- You will have time (recommended up to 2 hours) to prepare the task using reference materials. You can make notes and even write a draft. To actually take it ino the controlled assessment, you are allowed five bullet points of up to eight words each.
- Your teacher can discuss the task with you but cannot help you with the Spanish.
- Plan and organise your ideas.
- Make sure your writing meets the format, style, register and purpose of the task.
- Think about the Spanish you are going to show off.

3 Writing

- Use your notes to make sure you include all the ideas and language you need for a good grade.
- Build your writing out of Spanish you know.
- Write in proper sentences and paragraphs.
- Use connecting words to link your ideas logically.
- Put in different people's points of view. Use direct speech, or explain how you decided to do something. Make sure you talk about past and future as relevant to the task.
- Keep an eye on the time. You will have an hour to write 300 words.

4 Check

- Check your work several times looking at different features each time: masculine, feminine and plural, including adjectives.
- Verbs: infinitive, person, tense.
- Spelling, double letters (CaRoLiNe), and accents.
- Make sure you have put in opinions, connecting words, tenses, timewords, adjectives, intensifiers.

lo mejor es	odio	no aguanto	fui	iba a	voy a	el año pasado
hace dos días	sobre todo si	entonces	bastante	muy	realmente	

I just asked for two of everything, so I didn't have to worry about *un* or *una*.

Pronunciation

The pronunciation/spelling rules in Spanish are vital in all four assessments:
- in listening, you have to be able to turn the sound on the recording into a word in your head.
- in speaking, you have to pronounce Spanish accurately.
- in reading, you need to hear the words correctly in your head as you read.
- in writing, when you think of a word, you have to be able to write it down correctly.

The key features of Spanish spelling and pronunciation can be found in some of the very first Spanish you learn.

1 Spanish consonants – follow the rules 🔊 *Track 14*
Listen and read. What rules for the pronunciation of consonants are shown by the words in bold?

- **Hola**. ¿**Qué** tal?
- Bien, **gracias**. ¿Y tú?
- Muy bien ¿**Cómo** te **ll**amas?
- Me llamo **Javier**. ¿Y tú? ¿Cómo te llamas?
- Me llamo **Ángela**. ¿Eres **español**?
- No, soy de **Méjico**, pero vivo en España.
- ¿Cuántos años tienes?
- **Tengo** quince años.

z ce ci	soft c	diez, quince, cinco
j ge gi	soft g	ojos, geografía, ecologista
co ca cu	hard c	copiar, café, cuanto
go ga gu	hard g	tengo, garaje, haga
gua	"wa" sound	agua

Spanish vowels – keep it simple
Listen again. Now read these words out loud, paying attention to the pronunciation of the vowels.

| bien | y | tú | me | llamo | no | vivo | cuántos | tienes | quince |

Check your pronunciation
Read out the dialogue. Then listen and check your pronunciation.

2 Listen carefully
Listen. Write down the five words you hear correctly. 🔊 *Track 15*

3 If you hear it, you should be able to write it 🔊 *Track 16*
Listen. You will hear five words. Can you use the spelling rules to write down what your hear correctly.
- When there are two vowels together, pronounce them in the order they appear in the word:

siete	i...e...e	= siete
seis	e...i	= seis
cuatro	u...a...o	= cuatro
aunque	a...u...e	= aunque
ciudad	i...u...a	= ciudad
cuidado	u...i...a...o	= cuidado

4 **Ooh ah, ooh ah ah: u+a=ua**
Practise the words in bold (*siete*...) for exercise 3. Just say the vowels,
then say the whole word. Listen and check.

5 **Listen carefully, read carefully**　　　　　　　　　　🔊 *Track 17*
Listen carefully to the order of vowels and consonants. Listen and choose the word
you hear.

1	vine	viene	viento	veinte
2	vino	vine	viene	veinte
3	vino	vine	viento	veinte
4	viene	vine	viento	veinte
5	cuarto	cuatro	cuanto	encuentro
6	cuarto	cuatro	cuanto	encuentro
7	hablo	habla	hablar	hablan
8	hablo	habla	hablar	hablan

6 **Putting it all together**　　　　　　　　　　🔊 *Track 18*
Practise saying these words. Listen and check.

> salón garaje dormitorio cocina comedor sótano despacho

- If a word ends in a vowel, or 'n' or 's', the stress falls on the next to last syllable:
  casa restaurante mercado casas visitan viven

- If a word ends in a consonant (apart from 'n' or 's'), the stress falls on the last
  syllable: centro comercial hospital Madrid

- An accent can move the stress to a different syllable:
  jardín estación café Málaga

7 **Sounding Spanish**　　　　　　　　　　🔊 *Track 19*
Listen and practise copying:

¿Dónde está?
Me gusta hablar con mis amigos.
Me encanta el tenis.
Tengo otra hermana.

- Where one word ends in a vowel and the next word begins with a vowel,
  Spanish can run the two words into one sound.
- When a vowel is followed by an 'r' it is very tempting to lengthen the vowel as
  in the English word 'farmer'. In Spanish, the 'a' and the 'e' don't change:
  hermano: e...a...o = hermano
  hablar: a...a = hablar
- When an 'a' is followed by a 'y', be careful not to change the 'a' sound:
  playa: a...y...a = playa

Listening practice

Exercise 1-5 below are similar to the listening exercises you will do for the exam. The recordings to listen to are on the cd, and transcripts are on pages 13-14. The total mark that you can acheive for these exercises is 40. Good luck!

Exercise 1: questions 1–6

Penélope talks about her cinema-going habits. Read the questions. 🔊 *Track 20*
Listen to Penélope and answer the questions in English.

1 What does Penélope like to do at the weekend?_____ [1]
2 Whom does she go with?_____ [1]
3 Why didn't' she watch the horror film? _____ [1]
4 What did they watch instead? _____ [1]
5 What was the film about? _____ [1]
6 What does she think about the cinema in general?_____ [1]

Exercise 2: questions 7–11

🔊 *Track 21*

You are going to hear five people talking about their school. Read the list of words and the questions. Listen. For each question, write the correct two letters in the boxes.

A homework
B Thursdays
C future
D languages
E interesting
F important
G at weekends
H the teacher
I have fun
J seeing friends

7 Emilio likes ☐ because he likes ☐ . [1]

8 Verónica finds history ☐ but she doesn't think much of ☐ . [1]

9 Enrique doesn't like ☐ . He prefers to ☐ . [1]

10 Javier thinks school is ☐ for your ☐ . [1]

11 Ana thinks the most important thing is ☐ and she's not happy ☐ . [1]

Exercise 3: questions 12–19

🔊 *Track 22*

Chona talks about a trip she went on. Read the questions.
Listen to the recording and answer the questions in English.

12 When did she go camping? [1]

_____

13 How did her parents feel? [1]

_____

14 Why didn't they sleep much? [1]

_____

15 What was much better than in a city? [1]

_____

16 What can't you do where they were camping? [1]

_____

17 What will she have to make sure she does next time? [2]

_____

18 What do you have to learn to live without? [2]

_____

19 Why does she find beach holidays boring? [2]

_____

Exercise 4: questions 20–28

Track 23

Listen to Javier, Claudia and Elena talking about their town. Read the questions. For each question, tick the correct box.

20 He lives ... [1]

A	in a small town	
B	in a city	✓
C	in the countryside	

21 Javier likes where he lives because ... [1]

A	he likes the view.	
B	everything is close by.	
C	there are lots of people.	

22 The problem in the town is ... [1]

A	they used to clean, but not any more.	
B	they don't spend long enough cleaning.	
C	it doesn't stay clean.	

23 There's a problem because ... [1]

A	people don't care.	
B	there aren't any bins.	
C	there are roadworks.	

24 Claudia says where she lives ... [1]

A	it's the same situation.	
B	it's even worse.	
C	it's a nicer place.	

25 She says the tourists ...   [1]

A	are drunk.	
B	are dirty.	
C	make a mess.	

26 She thinks ...   [1]

A	school children drop paper.	
B	broken bottles are dangerous.	
C	three o'clock is very early.	

27 Elena says ...   [1]

A	they have to sort out living in such an expensive place.	
B	they are lucky to live there.	
C	instead of complaining they should clean up.	

28 She thinks the tourists ...   [1]

A	want to enjoy themselves.	
B	like the wildlife.	
C	are attractive.	

Exercise 5: questions 29–37   🔊 *Track 24*

Mateo is being interviewed about the opportunities for young people.
Read the questions. Listen to the interview and complete the notes in English.

29 The biggest problem is the lack of _____. [1]

30 In some parts of the country there are good universities, big companies and
_____. [1]

31 You may have to go to a city where _____. [1]

32 Mateo could _____. [1]

33 He is really talking about _____. [1]

34 He says people who already live in the city don't want _____. [1]

35 He wants the government to help _____. [1]

36 Other regions should be included in opportunities for _____. [1]

37 They should be considered for new projects like _____. [1]

Transcripts

Exercise 1 🔊 *Track 20*

Penélope:
Los fines de semana me gusta ir con mi novio al cine.

Penélope:
El sábado pasado yo quería ver una película de terror pero como a David no le gustan las películas de terror, decidimos ver ¿Qué queso es eso?, una película de dibujos animados.

Penélope:
Trata de las aventuras de dos ratones franceses que trabajan en un restaurante de París cuando llega una nueva cocinera de España. La película me encantó, aunque prefiero temas menos infantiles. Claro, también es importante divertirse y salimos muy contentos del cine, pero el próximo fin de semana quiero ver algo diferente. Si el sábado que viene volvemos al cine, no quiero ver otra comedia. David tendrá que ver lo que yo quiera.

Exercise 2 🔊 *Track 21*

Emilio:
Me gusta el instituto, sobre todo los jueves porque tengo inglés y francés. Pero no me gustan las ciencias.

Verónica:
Mi asignatura favorita es la historia. Me interesa mucho, pero el profesor es malo. Llega tarde y no prepara las clases.

Enrique:
El instituto está bien, pero no veo por qué tenemos que estudiar también en casa. Para mí la tarde es para disfrutarla con los amigos.

Javier:
El instituto es importante si quieres un buen trabajo. Sin educación no puedes salir adelante en la vida.

Ana:
Para mí, lo más importante del instituto es ver a los amigos. Podemos hablar o estudiar juntos, luego el fin de semana, no veo a nadie. Es muy triste.

Exercise 3 🔊 *Track 22*

Hace tres meses salí con unos amigos a acampar en el bosque. Lo pasamos muy bien, aunque mis padres estaban preocupados.

No estábamos lejos del pueblo, y no dormimos mucho – pasamos la noche a hablar. Hacía frío, pero afortunadamente no llovía y había un cielo sin nubes y una luna muy grande. Se veían las estrellas mucho mejor que en la ciudad.

Lo malo es que no se puede hacer fuego en el bosque, porque hay un riesgo muy alto de incendio, pero llevamos linternas.

La próxima vez voy a tener que pensar en comprar nuevas pilas, porque mi linterna no funcionaba muy bien.

Es importante aprender a vivir en el campo, hoy mucha gente no sabe vivir sin electricidad. Un día quiero ir a hacer una excursión organizada en la montaña, en el Pirineo, por ejemplo.

Las vacaciones en la playa me parecen bastante aburridas, siempre lo mismo, sin experiencias nuevas.

Exercise 4 🔊 *Track 23*

Javier:
Donde yo vivo, me gusta porque todo está allí, no hay por qué ir más lejos, pero el problema es que hay tanta gente. Eso no me molesta, excepto que luego tiran mucha basura en la calle. Pasan a limpiar, y al cabo de cinco minutos, todo está sucio otra vez. Hay cubos para basura, pero lo que pasa es que a la gente, no le importa. Como muchos no viven aquí, y ven que los trabajadores limpian la calle, piensan que tienen el derecho de tirar sus papeles allí.

Claudia:
Donde vivo yo, es aun peor la situación. Los turistas salen a las tres de la madrugada de los bares y también ensucian, pero son vasos y botellas que tiran. Claro, por la mañana cuando sales para ir al instituto, hay botellas rotas por todas partes. Claro la basura es desagradable, pero el vidrio es mucho más peligroso que los papeles.

Elena:
Tenemos suerte de vivir en un lugar tan precioso, que tanta gente quiere visitar. Hay que resolver los problemas, si no la vida se hace imposible para nosotros, y también la ciudad se hace menos atractiva para los turistas. Vienen a disfrutarse y es importante la vida nocturna, pero si la ciudad se pone más fea, irán a otro lugar. Tal vez es lo que vosotros queréis, pero sería una lástima.

Exercise 5   🎙 *Track 24*

¿Qué es lo más urgente cuando se trata del futuro de los jóvenes?
Lo que más nos preocupa es la falta de igualdad. En algunas partes del país, todo va bien. Hay universidades buenas, hay empresas grandes, hay trabajo. Pero si donde vives no hay oportunidades, ¿qué puedes hacer? ¿Pasarte la vida allí sin trabajo o con grandes dificultades para encontrar trabajo? ¿O irte a vivir en un lugar extraño donde no conoces a nadie?

No es una decisión muy fácil. ¿Qué piensas hacer?
Pues, para mí no sería tan difícil ir a vivir en Zaragoza, tengo familia allí y conozco la ciudad. Pero no estoy hablando de mi situación personal, sino lo que necesitamos todos los jóvenes para una vida mejor.

Entonces, ¿qué es lo que pedís?
No todo el mundo puede ir a vivir en las ciudades. A los que ya viven allí no les gusta. Y no podemos dejar morir al resto del país. Queremos que el gobierno ayude toda nuestra región. Cuando hay nuevas iniciativas, nuevas instalaciones culturales, oportunidades para industria y comercio, cuando hay proyectos para carreteras o aeropuertos... hay que pensar en otras ciudades e incluir a otras partes de la región.

Exercise 1, page 18   🎙 *Track 25*

1 afueras	6 hermano
2 taquilla	7 brazo
3 zapato	8 pierna
4 chaqueta	9 traje de baño
5 ingeniero	10 despeinado

Vocabulary in practice

Learning nouns and adjectives

Deciding what words to concentrate on

Do the exercises on this page. Then look at the vocabulary page for the unit you are studying or revising. Use one of the three activities to help you focus on which words to learn.

1 Check the meaning of these words (👆 see Students' Book, page 26), then traffic light them.
Green = I already know it
Orange = I could have guessed it
Red = I need to learn that word

el campo camp ☑	la cara face ☐	la finca farm ☐
la nariz nose ☐	un/a novio/a bf ☐	los ojos eyes ☑
delgado ☐	mayor ☐	mismo same ☐
redondo round ☐	vago ☐	un espejo mirror ☐
los muebles ☐ furniture	la ventana ☐ window	el equipo ☑ equipment

2 Check the meaning of these words. Some are on 👆 page 58 of the Students' Book.

• Now underline the ones that you would learn first for the topic "parts of the body".

• Put a ring round any words you think might be the examiner's favourites – ones that you have to learn because you could never guess them.

• Highlight any words that you like the sound of or that make you laugh.

el tobillo ankle	la cabeza	muerto
el brazo	el pie	el codo
el dedo gordo	la mano	la espalda
la garganta	el hombro	la muela
la nariz	el ojo eye	la pierna
el ombligo	el estómago stomach	

3 Check the meaning of these words (👆 see Students' Book, page 42). Put them into logical groups to help you learn them.

las afueras	bello	los jóvenes
el casco histórico	precioso	sucio
la plaza	un barco	un billete
un viaje	un bosque	ruidoso
la calle	hermoso	un avión
una taquilla	un tren	un pueblo

Strategies for learning

cow thirteen–calcetín = socks

thin tall Ron–cinturón = belt

1 The picture of the Cow Thirteen wearing socks is to remind you that calcetín means sock. Now draw pictures to help you remember the sound and meaning of these words.

camisa	bragas	zapato	falda	corbata

2 Use the clues that are in the word itself. It may be similar to another word you know in Spanish or in English.
- Write the word (in Spanish or English) that is a clue to the meaning of these words.
- Circle the ones where the clue could fool you into getting the word wrong.

Example: Pantalón – means trousers, but looks like 'pants'!

pantalón	blusa	chaqueta	suéter	traje de baño
sombrero	vestido	sostén	camiseta	

3 Learn the meaning of these words:
- carefully copy the Spanish down the side of a piece of paper,
- now write the English in a column next to it,
- fold the Spanish words away so you are looking at the English words,
- try to write the Spanish words correctly,
- open out the paper and check your spelling,
- carry on across the page, until you can spell all the words.

See Students' Book, page 58.

ruedas	merienda	buceo
carrera	almuerzo	buzo
palmarés	perezoso	césped
despeinado	consejo	espeleología

4 Put Spanish labels on things around your house or put Spanish words where you will keep seeing them. Which of these words would it help to see labelled?

puerta	ventana	cortina	hermano	gato	nevera
escalera	cama	alfombra	ropa	pared	cuadro

5 Make a card game to test yourself or play against a partner.

fontanero	camionero	electricista	cocinero	pescador	soldado
obrero	granjero	cura	jefe	ingeniero	secretaria
jardinero	periodista	autor	piloto	médico	enfermero

6 Try out these strategies on the vocabulary you are learning or revising. Evaluate which has most impact for you.

Testing yourself

1 Listen to the ten words on the CD. Can you write them accurately   🎵 *Track 25*
in Spanish? When you are testing yourself, get someone to read words to you
and see if you can spell them. Then write the English next to them.
Example: *afueras* – outskirts

2 Testing understanding. Write the English words for:

1	bragas _____	**6**	vago _____
2	consejo _____	**7**	cara _____
3	escalera _____	**8**	muebles _____
4	nevera _____	**9**	novio _____
5	redondo _____	**10**	cortina _____

3 Write the Spanish for:

1 foot _____

2 ticket _____

3 carpet _____

4 wall _____

5 T-shirt _____

Learning verbs

Noticing verbs

Don't make the mistake of just learning nouns!

1 Pick out the verbs from this list.

alto	tener éxito	mezclar	delgado	tengo	ducharse
tarde	vestirse	aburrirse	aspirar a	la edad	

2 🔍 Look at the unit vocabulary page in the Students' Book for the topic you
are studying or revising. How many of the words on the page are verbs?

Organise your learning

Learn the verb in the infinitive.

1 Draw arrows to match each verb in the left-hand column to its infinitive in the
right-hand column.

tengo	jugar (radical changing)
me llamo	hablar (regular)
voy	vivir (regular)
juego	tener (irregular)
hablé	llamarse (reflexive)
vivía	ir (irregular)

2 Separate these verbs into -ar, -er, -ir verbs, reflexive verbs, radical changing verbs or irregular verbs. Some will go in more than one list!

comer	jugar	hablar	decir	ir
volver	vestirse	tener	practicar	decidir
vivir	copiar	ducharse		

3 Keep a list of verbs useful for each topic, plus a list of those that are always going to be useful. How would you organise these verbs?

lavarse	ayudar	copiar	trabajar	escuchar	ir	tener	comer
viajar	bailar	romper	llegar	volar	nadar	leer	

Memorising verbs

1 Look back at the strategies you used for memorising nouns on page 16. Pick one of the strategies to help you learn each of the following verbs:
🖱 see Students' Book, page 26.

maquillarse	madrugar	tener hambre	llevarse bien
con	aconsejar	tomar una copa	parecerse a

2 Which of these verbs do you think you will need to use, and which do you think you will just need to recognise? Which will you use in fixed expressions, and which will you need to conjugate for yourself? 🕐 See Students' Book, page 42.

echar de menos	recordar	cruzar	seguir
cambiar	salir	caminar	hacer autostop

3 When learning verbs, you can use action and movement to try to fix the meaning in your mind. Practise miming and saying these verbs at the same time.

nadar	jugar	caminar	correr	escribir	leer

Recognising verbs

1 When reading or listening, it is important you recognise verbs you know, even if their ending has changed. Underline these verbs in the text.

salir	quedarse	decidir	ir	ver	pasar	llover	ser

El fin de semana pasado ibamos a ir a la playa, pero decidimos quedarnos en casa y pasamos toda la tarde viendo la televisión. De todas formas, no me gusta cuando llueve, es mejor no salir.

2 Find all the verbs in the following text. What does the end of the verb tell you? What is the infinitive? What does it mean in the text?

Prefiero estudiar en mi casa, porque los otros chicos hacen demasiado ruido en el instituto. Luego el profesor tiene que gritarles, y al final resulta que hay más ruido. Sólo trabajo muy cuando estoy bien tranquila y puedo concentrarme.

Learning high frequency words

When learning vocabulary, keep a separate list of words that are useful for any topic. Revise these words as often as you can.

Learning the 'little words'

1 Match the 'little words' in box A with the English in box B.

A
| un |
| al |
| yo |
| mis |
| de |
| las |
| una |
| a |
| mi |
| los |
| del |
| la |
| me |
| el |

B
| to |
| the (m) |
| the (m) |
| the (f) |
| the (m plural) |
| the (f plural) |
| a (m) |
| a (f) |
| my |
| my (plural) |
| me |
| I |
| of or from |
| of the (m) |
| at or to |

2 Watch out for expressions where the 'little' words are slightly different in Spanish. Translate literally, then correctly, as in the example.

Example: *Juego **al** tenis = I play at the tennis = I play tennis*

1 Es el dormitorio **de** mis padres. _____

_____

2 Me gustan **las** fresas. _____

_____

3 Son **las** seis. _____

_____

4 Me duele **la** cabeza. _____

_____

5 **Me** llamo Carla. _____

_____

6 **El** sábado no tengo clases. _____

_____

3 Complete the sentences with 'little words'.

_____ hermano juega _____ golf _____ fin de semana, pero _____ prefiero quedarme en _____ dormitorio y hablar con _____ amigos por teléfono. No _____ interesa _____ deporte.

Learning connecting words

1 Copy the grid and organise these connecting words in it.

Adding information or examples	Giving reasons or explaining	Contrasting or alternatives	Sequencing or narrating

y	porque	sobre todo si	sin embargo	aunque
luego	también	además	primero	después
por ejemplo	entonces	así que	puesto que	pues
cuando	donde	que	pero	mientras
en lugar de	en vez de	o		

2 Use an appropriate connective word from the list below to complete the text. The first one has been done for you.

o	sobre todo si	en lugar de	por ejemplo	pero
y	donde	adonde	~~entonces~~	

Si hace sol <u>entonces</u> prefiero ir a la playa, _____ puedo ir con mi familia, _____ el fin de semana fuimos por la tarde _____ ir de compras. _____ si llueve, prefiero ir a la ciudad_____ puedes ir a un museo _____ un café. _____ mañana quiero ir al centro _____ tomar un café.

Time words

1 A good grade in all four skills depends on being able to refer to different frames. Categorise these words according to whether they refer to present, past, or future.

ayer	anteayer	mañana	pasado mañana	hoy	ahora	antes
el fin de semana próxima		algún día	hace dos días		el año pasado	

2 Narrating events or giving instructions require time words. Put these into groups of words that you could use together in a sequence:

primero	en ocasiones especiales	muchas veces	a veces
pocas veces	rara vez	luego	después	finalmente	nunca
	siempre	cada fin de semana	normalmente

3 Write sentences using your sequence of words.
Example: Primero hay que ir todo recto, luego a la izquierda ...

Question words

1 Check you know the meaning of these words.

> qué dónde cuándo cuánto por qué cómo cuál quién

2 Use the correct word to start each question. Then answer the questions in Spanish.

1 ¿_____ vives?
2 ¿_____ dinero ganas por hora?
3 ¿_____ no te gusta vivir aquí?
4 ¿_____ es tu asignatura favorita?
5 ¿A_____ hora sale el tren?
6 ¿_____ vas al instituto?
7 ¿_____ vive en tu casa contigo?
8 ¿_____ es tu cumpleaños?

Organising high frequency words

1 Keep a list of words that are useful for not just one topic but for all topics. Look at these words. Which are words that are always going to be useful?

> pan si todo casa todavía nadie coche ardilla

2 Look at the unit vocabulary page for the topic you are studying or revising. How many of the words are useful for any topic? Put them in a separate list.

Learning expressions and structures

Opinion words

1 Organise opinions in the box below into positive and negative.

2 Organise them according to their structure: first person verb, impersonal verb, adjective, etc.

3 Make a list of the ones that would normally be followed by an infinitive.

4 Make separate lists of ones that are usually linked to a specific topic, e.g people or places.

me gusta	me encanta	odio	no aguanto
me interesa	no me gusta	es simpático	es agradable
es antipático	me fascina	me molesta	prefiero
lo mejor es	me da asco	es delicioso	mi favorito es

5 Show off a range of opinions to talk about these things.

Talking about the future

1 Match the Spanish in the left-hand column with its English translation in the right-hand column.

Mi sueño es ...	My plan is to ...
Voy a ...	The best thing would be to ...
Iba a ...	I hope to ...
Quiero ...	My dream is to ...
Mi proyecto es de ...	I am going to ...
Lo mejor sería ...	I am going to ...
Espero ...	I want to ...
	My plan is to ...

2 Use the expressions from exercise 1 to rewrite the text below.
Avoid repeating *voy a*:

En las vacaciones voy a ir a España. Voy a ir a Málaga y voy a ir a la playa. Voy a alojarme en un hotel de lujo y voy a comer platos españoles en el restaurante. Voy a hablar español porque voy a hacer nuevos amigos en España.

_____

_____

Getting what you want

1 Do you know the Spanish for ...?

I want_____ I would like_____ I need _____ Give me _____

Please _____ Thank you _____ Do you have?_____ Is there?_____

2 Use these expressions to ask for the following.

3 Finish these questions using the pictures:

   1 ¿Dónde está ..._____ ?

   2 ¿A qué hora ... _____ ?

   3 ¿Puedo ..._____ ?

   4 ¿Está abierto ..._____ ?

   5 ¿Está lejos ..._____ ?

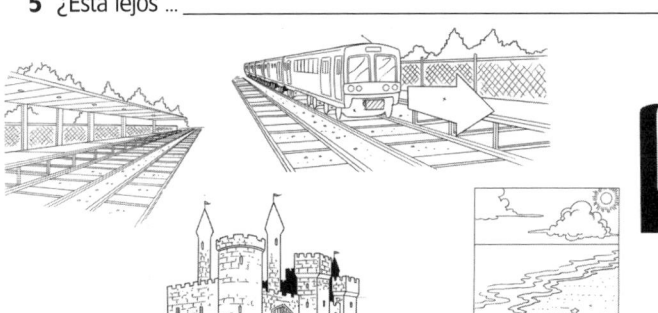 

Unit 1A Mi vida

Escenario: Oral

Students' Book page 25

Interview a family member

Interview the family member of a contestant on *Telón Abierto*.

Preparing the task

1 You will have time to prepare the task using the Students' Book.
Make brief notes and practise what you are going to do.

2 Research information on Isadora and Lorena in Unit 1A.
Decide which family member is going to be interviewed. Make a list of possible questions, covering all the parts of the task:

- personality,
- likes and interests,
- how they get on,
- routine,
- who they take after,
- jobs around the house.

3 Use verbs in the third person.
Make sure you are good at using them to talk about the contestant, and make sure you know how to say 'he likes' / 'she likes'.

4 Practise the task with the list of questions and the Students' Book to help you.
Use fillers to keep talking while you come up with an answer. You can make five bullet points of eight words each (maximum) to help you, but it is better if you sound as if you are really responding to the questions.

Performing the task

Try to record the interview in one take. It needs to sound natural rather than scripted. Use your fillers if you get stuck. If your teacher is using this as a practice for the real assessments, then get used to thinking on your feet and keep talking!

Escenario: Escrito

Students' Book page 25

Write a horoscope

Write a horoscope style personality description for Jorge, Mari Ángeles, Lorena or Isidoro. Then write a letter to explain a personal problem the character has.

Preparing the task

1 You will have time to use the Student's Book to prepare. First, think about the skills and grammar you will need to complete the task:

- personal details
- description
- personality
- interests
- problem

> adjectives   present tense   reflexive verbs
> opinions   connecting words
> future with 'going to' verb + infinitive
> indirect speech (he says that...)

2 Choose one of the characters from Unit 1A. Research what you need to know about them, and imagine the rest!

3 Plan the different sections of the horoscope style description, making sure you show off the Spanish you have been learning.

4 Write in full sentences and try to link your ideas so that the overall description reads like something you would find in a magazine.

5 Look at page 21 of the Students' Book for ideas of how to use your Spanish to write a letter.
Let the problem emerge from the Spanish you know. Don't think of a crazy problem and then find you can't say it.

6 Little personal details about a famous TV contestant. You know the sort of things magazines love:

- who they get on with
- who they take after
- what household jobs they do
- their routine...

You can make five bullet points of eight words each (maximum) to remind you of important points.

Writing the task

This is when you realise how important it is to plan the task using Spanish you know! Keep it simple, and find ways to bring in everything you can remember.
You can use a dictionary to check words, but don't use it to try to write things you haven't learnt.
Keep an eye on the clock and manage your time efficiently.
When you have finished, check your work following the advice on page 7 of this book.

Gramática en acción

Students' Book page 22

1 Masculine, feminine, singular, plural. Complete the text with the correct form of the words in the box.

un	moderno	pequeño	de + el	el	mi
mi	mi	alegre	el	frustrado	un

Vivo en un? / una? piso _____ en una ciudad_____
cerca _____ mar. Me gustaría tener _____
casa en _____ campo con _____
jardín. Vivo con _____ hermanas y _____
padre. Ellas son muy _____ pero _____
padre está _____ .

2 Choose the correct plural for these words. There is one correct answer hiding in each column.

hotel	jardín	salón	cuarto de baño	grande
hotels	jardines	salónes	cuarto de baños	grans
hotéles	jardins	salons	cuartos de baño	grands
hoteles	jardíns	salons	cuartos de baños	grands
hótels	jardínes	salones	cuartos des baños	gran
hostels	járdins	sálons	cuarto de baño	grandes

3 Tick the box or boxes that correctly describe these verbs.

	Regular	Reflexive	Radical changing	Irregular
comer	☐	☐	☐	☐
jugar	☐	☐	☐	☐
vivir	☐	☐	☐	☐
ir	☐	☐	☐	☐
vestirse	☐	☐	☐	☐
preferir	☐	☐	☐	☐
tener	☐	☐	☐	☐
levantarse	☐	☐	☐	☐

4 Complete the sentences with the correct form of *ser* or *tener*.

1 Mi hermano _____ muy inteligente.
2 Mis hermanas _____ delgadas.
3 Mi padre _____ cuarenta años.
4 Mi hermano _____ un perro y dos conejos.
5 Mis padres _____ un ordenador en su dormitorio.
6 Yo _____ demasiado joven para ver ese programa.
7 Yo_____ un hermano mayor.
8 Yo _____ el mayor.

5 Translate into Spanish using the verbs in parentheses.

1 Do you wear a uniform to school? (llevar)
2 We prefer to have breakfast later. (preferir)
3 How do you go to school? (ir)
4 What time do you wake up? (despertarse)
5 They enjoy themselves. (divertirse)

6 Complete the questions with the missing question word.

1 ¿_____ vive aquí?
2 ¿De _____ es este dormitorio?
3 ¿_____ hay un pelo en mi sopa?
4 ¿_____ es mi dormitorio?
5 ¿_____ está mi dormitorio?
6 ¿_____ tías tienes?
7 ¿_____ es tu cumpleaños?

Checklist

This chart shows the topics, skills and grammar covered in Unit 1A. Use the symbols from the key to fill in the right-hand column of the table. This will help you to see what you need to spend some more time on.

Key

☺	I know/can do this very well
☺	I'm not too sure I know/can do this
☹	I don't know/cannot do this well enough

Unit 1A Mi vida I can ...	How confident am I?
... give basic personal details.	
... describe other people.	
... talk about my routine.	
... talk about household jobs.	
... talk about life in my family.	
... start a conversation.	
... keep a conversation going.	
... extend my sentences with connecting words.	
... ask questions.	
... check for accuracy.	
... tell the gender of common nouns.	
... use adjectives and make them agree.	
... use the present tense of regular verbs.	
... use reflexive verbs.	
... use radical changing verbs.	
... use 'going to' to talk about the future.	

Unit 1B Nuestro entorno

Escenario: Oral

Students' Book page 41

Act out sketch

A tourist asks for directions but ends up totally confused.

Preparing the task

You can plan and prepare the task together, but remember for top grades, there needs to be evidence of spontaneity and dealing with the unexpected. It will also sound better if you are acting, not regurgitating a script.

1 The traveller will have to prepare his questions. The others could each specialise in a different form of transport.
- Pages 34–35 in the Student Book will give you lots of ideas for language and information on travel in Spain.
- You should also think about adding in personal experience to make sure you include past and future: 'Well, when I went to Madrid...' 'I'm going to Madrid, but I'm not going to...'

2 Structure the whole scene around the questions.
- Practise improvising with the Student's Book open at page 34.
- When one person runs out of ideas, someone else can join in.

Do I need to ...?	When ...?
Can I ...?	Where ...?
Do I have to ...?	Is it worth ...?
Is it quicker/cheaper/easier to ...?	Do I go ...?
Where can I ...?	Is there ...?

3 Plan how you think it could end:
- they get revenge, by giving him so much information he finally has no more questions.
- he just gets worse, questioning and correcting the information they give.
- they end up arguing with each other and ignore him.
- it builds up and then dies away to nothing
- make it a competition to see who runs out of steam first.

4 Make notes to make sure you remember some of your points.

These will just be 5 bullet points maximum 8 words each, not a script. It would be useful to have a checklist of some of the language you want to use to get a higher grade: opinions, past, future, connecting words, sentences with "if"...

Performing the task

Try to make it feel real and spontaneous. If you get stuck or forget something, make it up or use one of the fillers you practised in Unit 1A. If someone else goes wrong or does something unexpected, respond to the situation and keep going. Have your notes available for emergencies, but try to do without them. If you are being filmed then you will have to do some acting. Even if it is just a voice recording, then acting will come across in the pace and expression of what you say.

Escenario: Escrito

Students' Book page 41

Write an email in Spanish
Write an email to a Spanish friend who is coming to visit.

Preparing the task

1 Think about the skills and grammar you will need to complete the task:

> opinion words
>
> comparatives/superlatives
>
> connecting words/time words
>
> preterite to talk about your experience of their town or transport
>
> imperfect for what their town was like
>
> future with 'you are going to'
>
> verb + infinitive: you can, you have to, you need to
>
> adjectives and descriptions

2 You will have time to prepare the task.
Plan ways to use all the elements of your toolkit in this task:

- make sure you can use the second person (tú form) of verbs to say 'when **you** visit ... **you** can ... you have to ...'
- you can only make five bullet points of eight (maximum) words each into the exam, but you can plan far more in your head using your Students' Book.

3 Think about each part of the task and the language it is going to use:

- **transport**: description, comparison, personal past experience, you can ...
- **directions**: you have to, you are going to, you can, I am going to, if you want to ...
- **description**: it is, there is, you can ...
- **comparison**: when I went, it was, there was, more, less ...

4 Plan how to make the whole piece of writing link together and sound personal and real:

- organisation
- logic
- connecting words
- opinions
- past experience

Writing the task

Don't get stuck trying to think of fancy starter sentences. Get straight in to 'when you visit ...' and then build an answer out of Spanish you know. Use your notes to make sure you include everything you want to. Check your work following the advice on page 7 of this book.

Gramática en acción

Students' Book page 38

1 Translate into Spanish.

I went to Spain, I swam in the sea, I ate in a restaurant, I visited a castle.

_____

_____

I made new friends, I drank in a bar, I danced in the street, I spent too much money.

_____

_____

2 Say what person of the verb is being used. Translate the verb into English.

1 Fuimos a España. _____

2 Decidió hacer camping. _____

3 Dije, 'Gracias, me gusta mucho.' _____

4 Comieron platos típicos. _____

5 Nadamos en la piscina. _____

3 Write down the tense of each verb and translate the sentences into English.

1 Mi madre vivía en Colombia. _____

_____

2 Nado en el mar. _____

_____

3 Nadó en la piscina. _____

_____

4 Bebemos agua mineral. _____

_____

5 Hice castillos de arena. _____

_____

6 Viajábamos mucho. _____

_____

7 Bebimos en un bar. _____

_____

4 Complete these sentences with *ser* or *estar*.

1 Mi casa _____ muy grande.

2 Mi casa _____ muy sucia.

3 Mi casa _____ en el centro de la ciudad.

4 Ahora _____ en mi casa.

5 Translate these sentences into Spanish.

1 My new house is bigger than my old flat. _____

2 I used to live in a bigger house. _____

3 When I was younger, I wanted to travel. _____

4 The city isn't as exciting (emocionante) as it used to be. _____

_____

5 I would like to live somewhere quieter. _____

6 Travelling by bus in Mexico is quicker than travelling by train. _____

_____

Checklist

This chart shows the topics, skills and grammar covered in Unit 1B. Use the symbols from the key to fill in the right-hand column of the table. This will help you to see what you need to spend some more time on.

Key

☺	I know/can do this very well
☺	I'm not too sure I know/can do this
☹	I don't know/cannot do this well enough

Unit 1B Nuestro entorno I can ...	How confident am I?
... describe where I live.	
... compare different places.	
... ask for information about a town.	
... sort out transport problems.	
... describe a journey.	
... understand when to use *tú* and *usted*.	
... use the preterite to say what happened.	
... use the imperfect to say what used to happen.	
... use the comparative and the superlative.	
... use strategies to pick out what I can understand from text.	
... use strategies to keep track when listening.	
... use the most efficient strategies to learn vocabulary.	

Unit 2A Una vida sana y activa

Escenario: Oral

Students' Book page 57

Promote healthy living
Create a television advert promoting healthy living.

Preparing the task

1 Decide how serious your advert is going to be:
- an old fashioned black and white film with a patronising commentary,
- a modern ironic sketch with a twist in the tail,
- an annoying song that will stick in people's heads.

2 Prepare the task using the Students' Book. Look at everything you have done and decide how to use it:
- talking about what sports you like/don't like,
- famous sports personalities and role models,
- healthy (and unhealthy) lifestyles,
- injuries and accidents.

3 Feature a healthy and an unhealthy person.
One idea would be to feature a healthy person and an unhealthy person, but of course the healthy person has an unfortunate accident while exercising, or chokes on a carrot.

4 For a top mark, make sure you are prepared to improvise and expand.
You can plan and rehearse your film. Decide on your roles and plan the overall structure. When you practise, try to add different details each time. You can make five bullet points of eight words maximum to help you remember what to say, or to remind you of the language points you need for a good mark.

Performing the task

Try to film or record it in one take. If it sounds a little bit dodgy, remember that in your assessed task you need to sound as if you are reacting spontaneously. You are not aiming to be 100% word perfect!
Use your connecting words to link and expand your ideas. Use the routine opinion → reason → example in the past/future to keep talking and to make sure you use the sort of language that will get you a good mark.

Escenario: Escrito

⬤ Students' Book page 57

Sporting holiday

Imagine you went to an activity centre. Write a diary entry about what you did on one particular day of your sporting holiday.

Preparing the task

1 Think about the skills and grammar you will need to complete the task:

- opinions,
- preterite tense for what you did earlier,
- perfect tense for what has happened today,
- connecting words and time words,
- intensifiers and techniques for adding colour and drama.

2 Match the Spanish you have to each part of the task.

> **Talking about the incident**
> The imperfect to say what was happening
> The perfect to say what has happened
> The preterite to say what happened
> Time words and intensifiers
> Direct speech: I said' 'she said'

> **Talking about the day**
> The activities you can do
> Your opinion of them
> Some safety aspects
> What you did before the incident

> **Saying what you did to help**
> Some verbs in the first person
> preterite: I went, I helped, I said ...

3 Plan carefully. Make sure your diary entry doesn't just turn into a list of things that happened.
You can make five bullet points of eight words maximum to remind you of your plan or to help you remember some of the important language points you want to put in to get a good mark.

Writing the task

Build your writing out of Spanish you know. Only use your dictionary to check single words. Structure your work as you planned, and include the language you want to show off for a good grade.
Check your work following the advice on page 7 of this book.

Gramática en acción

⬤ Students' Book page 54

1 Write the correct form of the verb beside its English translation.

hablar		jugar	
I talk	_____	I play	_____
I talked	_____	I played	_____
She talks	_____	He plays	_____
She talked	_____	He played	_____

hacer		ir	
I do	_____	I go	_____
I did	_____	I went	_____
She does	_____	She goes	_____
She did	_____	She went	_____

2 Choose the correct form of the verb in each sentence.

1 Me gusta / gustan montar a caballo.
2 Me gusta / gustan la equitación.
3 Me gusta / gustan los caballos.
4 Me encanta / encantan la natación.
5 Me encanta / encantan nadar.
6 Me encanta / encantan el deporte.
7 Me encanta / encantan los deportes.

3 Translate these sentences into Spanish.

1 Do you like football? (gustar)

_____

2 Does your leg hurt? (doler)

_____

3 How does that seem to you? (parecer)

_____

4 I like many different sports. (gustar)

_____

5 Sports don't interest me. (interesar)

_____

6 Tennis doesn't interest me. (interesar)

_____

4 Translate the text into English, paying attention to structures with *se*.

Se pueden hacer muchos deportes diferentes. Se puede nadar en la piscina y hay un campo donde se juega al fútbol o al hockey. En el invierno se hace esquí, y en el centro se tiene todo lo necesario incluyendo botas y cascos.

_____

_____

_____

5 Complete these sentences choosing *he* or *tengo*.

1 _____ una bicicleta.
2 _____ quince años.
3 No_____ tiempo para hacer ejercicio.
4 Me_____ torcido el tobillo.
5 No_____ jugado al rugby mucho.
6 _____ que ir al parque.
7 _____ comido demasiado.
8 _____ un dolor de cabeza.

Checklist

This chart shows the topics, skills and grammar covered in Unit 2A. Use the symbols from the key to fill in the right-hand column of the table. This will help you to see what you need to spend some more time on.

Key

☺	I know/can do this very well
😐	I'm not too sure I know/can do this
☹	I don't know/cannot do this well enough

Unit 2A Una vida sana y activa I can ...	How confident am I?
... talk about which sport I prefer.	
... compare role models in the past and now.	
... talk about healthy lifestyles.	
... explain about injuries and illness.	
... talk about different outdoor activities.	
... use intensifiers to sound more convincing.	
... link sentences with connecting words.	
... use impersonal verbs like *me interesa*.	
... use reflexive constructions like *se juega*.	
... use irregular forms of the preterite.	
... use time clauses like *desde hace*.	
... use the perfect tense.	
... use adverbs and phrases of time and place.	

Unit 2B Comer y beber

Escenario: Oral

Students' Book page 73

Interview a chef
A restaurant critic questions the chef and customers in a restaurant.

Preparing the task

1 The task will be structured round the critic's questions.
- For top marks, you should have some flexibility, responding spontaneously and extending your answers.
- You could try to introduce more interaction, with people interrupting to contradict or support each other.
- Make sure you prepare the basic language to do the task, and think about ways to expand or make spontaneous comments as you go.

2 You will have time to prepare together using the Students' Book.
- Start by thinking about the questions. You will probably use the *usted* form as it is a formal interview. It will need to include questions about the past and possibly future plans.

3 Use the Students' Book to plan the parts of the task.
- The chef explains how to make his most famous dish. Perhaps he demonstrates it as he goes along, so he can use the present continuous. He could talk about what he is going to do next, or say what he used to do.
- The others can react and comment spontaneously with opinions or exclamations.

4 When the critic talks to the customers, they need to show off their opinions, describe food, and use the past to talk about the experience of eating in the restaurant.
- If they mention any problems, the chef might like to comment.

Performing the task

Focus on the main points and sequence of the task as you planned it. Be prepared to comment, expand, or respond flexibly. If someone gets stuck, the others should quickly carry on the conversation naturally.

Escenario: Escrito

Students' Book page 73

Write for the Michelin Guide
Write the webpage of a 3-star restaurant for the Michelin Guide.

Preparing for the task

1 You can use the internet.
Look at Spanish restaurant guides for ideas and design inspiration, but use the Students' Book to focus on your Spanish.

2 Think about the skills and grammar you will need to complete the task:
- **opinions**: verb + infinitive
- **adjectives**: comparisons/superlatives
- **present**: present continuous
- **preterite**: imperfect
- **connecting words**: intensifiers, time words, exclamations

3 Match the language in your toolkit to the parts of the task:

Biography of the chef
Descriptions
Preterite
Imperfect (used to)
Perfect (he has ...)

Information
Descriptions
Opinions
Verb + infinitive
Comparative/superlative

Customers' comments
Opinions
Comparative/superlative
Imperfect
Preterite
Future

4 Think carefully about which parts of the task are going to show off your Spanish at the right level.
The customers' comments are a great opportunity to talk about their opinions, their experience of visiting the restaurant, and whether they would go again. Use connecting words and time words to link and extend your ideas. Plan carefully so that you cover the separate parts of the task, but also develop key parts to the right level of Spanish for a good grade.

Writing the task

Concentrate on the Spanish, within a general 'webpage' layout. Build your work out of Spanish you know. Make sure you follow your plan and develop the parts of the task where you can show off your Spanish. You can use a dictionary to check single words, but don't use Spanish you haven't learnt. Check your work carefully using the advice on page 7 of this book.

Gramática en acción

Students' Book page 70

1 Decide whether to use the infinitive or the gerund in these sentences.

  1 Me gusta <u>comer / comiendo</u> pastel.
  2 Estoy <u>preparar / preparando</u> la cena.
  3 Lo mejor es <u>beber / bebiendo</u> un refresco bien frío.
  4 Están <u>comprar / comprando</u> los ingredientes.
  5 No puedo hablar; estoy <u>comer /comiendo</u>.

2 Choose the correct word.

  1 Las dos hamburguesas, las patatas fritas, el helado y el café, son para <u>me / mi / mí</u>.
  2 Y para <u>tu / tú / ti / te</u>, ¿Qué te apetece?
  3 Hay dos pizzas para <u>nos / nosotros / nuestro</u>.
  4 Lo compré para <u>él / el / le</u>.
  5 Salí a comer con <u>la / ella / le</u>.

3 Make 4 silly and 4 sensible sentence using the words:

  Example: **Sensible** *Tienes que comprar un pastel.* **Silly** *Hay que cocinar el gato.*

Debes	comer	un pastel
Necesitas	beber	la ensalada
Tienes que ➡	comprar ➡	el gato
Hay que	cocinar	a tu hermano
No debes	ayudar	la limonada

4 Now translate these sentences into Spanish.

  1 This cake is the best. _____
  2 The best is cake. _____
  3 Cake is better than ice cream._____

5 Rewrite the text below without repeating *tienes que*.
Tienes que ir al supermercado. Tienes que comprar los ingredientes. Tienes que volver a la casa. Tienes que poner los ingredientes en la nevera.

6 Translate the text below into Spanish using *se* instead of they.
In Spain, they eat cereal and cake for breakfast. They heat up water in the microwave. They make tea with warm water. They eat breakfast very quickly and then they go out to work.

calentar – to heat up	el microondas – the microwave	caliente – warm

Checklist

This chart shows the topics, skills and grammar covered in Unit 2B. Use the symbols from the key to fill in the right-hand column of the table. This will help you to see what you need to spend some more time on.

Key

☺	I know/can do this very well
☺	I'm not too sure I know/can do this
☹	I don't know/cannot do this well enough

Unit 2B Comer y beber I can ...	How confident am I?
... talk about my favourite food.	
... talk about healthy food.	
... buy food in a shop.	
... order food in a restaurant.	
... sort out problems in a restaurant.	
... compare food and drink in different cultures.	
... use tone of voice to sound genuinely interested.	
... be polite.	
... make points for and against.	
... write numbers correctly.	
... use a range of expressions followed by the infinitive.	
... use *usted* correctly.	
... use pronouns after prepositions.	

Unit 3A Las fiestas

Escenario: Oral

Students' Book page 89

International party

Your Spanish teacher wants to organise an evening activity for your group and your exchange partners when they come. Prepare some answers to his/her questions. Don't forget to talk about your own past experience and how it went.

Preparing the task

1 Expand your answers.

There is a list of questions, but for a top grade, you are going to have to take the initiative and expand your answers. Take the questions as a starting point, but be prepared for the conversation to follow the ideas you come up with.

2 To start off, think of some ways of suggesting lots of different ideas:

> You can...   It would be best to...   You could...
> Why not...   I think...

3 Use expressions for inviting people.

Lots of the expressions you used for inviting people out are useful here.

4 Suggest places to go.

Use the Students' Book to make sure you can suggest lots of places to go. Explain the activities and give the details asked for in the suggested questions. Make a list of opinions you can use. For a top mark, make sure you talk about your personal past experience (preterite tense) or future plans. You can make five bullet points of eight words maximum, but you can plan plenty more in your head.

Performing the task

Make sure you extend your answers. Use your connecting words. To keep going, follow the routine: opinion → reason → example in the past/future. Listen carefully to the questions and be prepared for the conversation to develop naturally. Even in a voice recording, eye contact and hand gestures will help your pace and expression come across well.

Escenario: Escrito

Students' Book page 89

Special time

Write an email to Spanish friends who will be here during a special time of the year.
Tell them:

- what usually happens,
- what it was like last time,
- what you have planned.

Preparing the task

1 Think about the skills and grammar you will need to complete the task:

present tense	verb + infinitive	future expressions
preterite	imperfect	imperfect continuous
opinions	adjectives	comparatives/superlatives
connecting words	time words	direct speech

2 Use your Students' Book to find ways to use all the elements in your toolkit to complete the parts of the task saying:

- **what normally happens**: present tense, adjectives, comparatives/superlatives, time words, connecting words'
- **what it was like last time**: imperfect, combining imperfect continuous with preterite (I was ___ing when...), direct speech (I said, she said),
- **what you have planned**: future expressions.

3 Plan the overall structure of your email, and think of ways to make it sound personal and logical.

4 You can write down five bullet points of eight words (maximum) each, but you can plan far more in your head.
Use your bullet points to remember your overall plan, or as a checklist of the most important language points for a top mark.

Writing the task

Don't get stuck thinking of fancy starters. Get started by building an answer out of the Spanish you know.

Follow your plan and use your bullet points to make sure you put in all your ideas and language. Only use a dictionary to check single words, and don't start putting in things you haven't learnt.

Check your work using the advice on page 7 of this book.

Gramática en acción

🖱 Students' Book page 86

1 Underline the verbs which are in the continuous form of the imperfect (was---ing).

1 Comía en la cocina.
2 Estaba hablando con mis amigas.
3 Estaba organizando una fiesta.
4 Decidía qué hacer.
5 Estaba escuchando música.
6 Estaba bailando.

2 Put the underlined verbs into the preterite. Then use them to make sentences with your answers to question 1.

Example: Estaba comiendo en la cocina cuando mi amigo llegó.

1 Mi padre llamar por teléfono.

_____

2 Mi padre decir que tenía que terminar mis deberes.

_____

3 Empezar a llover.

_____

4 El gato comer se mi hamster.

_____

5 Mi hermana verme.

_____

3 Translate these sentences into English.

1 Lo compré para mi padre. _____
2 Es para ellos. _____
3 Te lo compré. _____
4 Voy a dárselo mañana. _____
5 ¿El gato? No es mío. _____

4 Translate these sentences into Spanish.

1 I saw a book, so I bought it for my sister. _____
2 If I see a cake, I have to eat it. _____
3 I want to buy it for you. _____
4 The balloons? I bought them. _____
5 The cakes? I didn't eat them. _____
6 He said that it was for me. _____

5 Choose *lo* or *lo* que. Then translate into English.

1 Lo / Lo que me gusta es divertirme. _____
2 Lo / Lo que más me gusta es relajarme. _____
3 Lo / Lo que mejor es relajarse en la casa. _____
4 Lo / Lo que más importante son los amigos. _____
5 Lo / Lo que necesito es salir más. _____

Checklist

This chart shows the topics, skills and grammar covered in Unit 3A. Use the symbols from the key to fill in the right-hand column of the table. This will help you to see what you need to spend some more time on.

Key

☺	I know/can do this very well
☺	I'm not too sure I know/can do this
☹	I don't know/cannot do this well enough

Unit 3A Las fiestas I can ...	How confident am I?
... arrange to go out.	
... organise a party.	
... talk about shopping.	
... describe a party.	
... describe a festival.	
... scan text for information.	
... spot red herrings when listening.	
... understand different sorts of pronoun.	
... use the continuous form of the imperfect.	

Unit 3B Cine y televisión

Escenario: Oral

Students' Book page 105

A film review
Working in groups of three, prepare a talk in Spanish about a film you have seen or the film *El Orfanato* described in the Students' Book.

Preparing the task

1 Think of the Spanish you will need to use for each part of the task:

The actors:
- adjectives,
- present tense,
- comparatives/superlatives,
- imperfect (what they used to do),
- preterite (things they did).

The plot:
- preterite (what happened),
- imperfect (what was happening),
- time words and connecting words.

Evaluation:
- opinions,
- speech (my friend said...),

- adjectives,
- comparatives/superlatives.

2 Don't spend too long arguing about which film to choose.
Pick one and then spend the time on research and preparation. In your research you may find some useful vocabulary and expressions, but be careful to build your presentation out of the Spanish you know.

3 Co-ordinate your group's work.
Make sure you are not repeating information and that each section is going to keep the audience's interest. You can prepare visual material to help make your presentation interesting, for example using ICT.

Performing the task

Concentrate on giving information to your audience.
Make eye contact and use your body language to emphasise your points. This will also help you speak at the right pace. Don't just pour out the words you prepared. Think about what you are trying to communicate and use your Spanish to get it across.

Escenario: Escrito

Students' Book page 105

A festival
Research the Benicàssim Festival (or any other festival, if you prefer).

Preparing the task

1 Think about the skills and grammar you will need to complete the task:

> present tense
> preterite
> connecting words
> opinions
> time words
> verb + infinitive
>
> perfect
> imperfect
> adjectives
> future expressions
> comparative
> superlative

2 Think about how to break down the task to show off your Spanish:

> **Give basic information**
> Present
> Preterite
> Adjectives
> Comparative/superlative

> **Quote people with different view points**
> Opinions
> Verb + infinitive

> **Write as if you have been there**
> Preterite
> Imperfect
> Adjectives
> Time words

> **Write about the next festival**
> Future expressions

3 Research enough facts to be able to develop each of your sections.
You will find some useful vocabulary in your research, but build it into sentences that use the Spanish you know. Page 105 in the Students' Book has some information about the festival. You can use this information to prepare. When you are writing up the assessment you can only have five bullet points of eight words (maximum) to remind you of important points.

Writing the task

Build the letter out of the Spanish you know. Use your dictionary to check words, but not to write whole sentences. Use the advice on page 7 of this booklet to check your work

Gramática en acción

Students' Book page 102

1 Match up these verbs in the preterite with their infinitive.

tuve	ser
estuve	dar
dijo	ir
fui	decir
pusimos	estar
dieron	tener
fui	poner

2 Use the verbs in exercise 1 to complete these sentences.

1 _____ el premio a la mejor actriz.

2 _____ que era una experiencia inolvidable.

3 _____ que confesar que no me gustó su canción.

4 _____ a punto de llorar.

5 _____ el disco y bailamos.

6 _____ al concierto.

7 _____ la primera persona que escuchó la canción.

3 Translate these sentences into Spanish.

1 We didn't see anybody famous.

_____

2 We didn't like the music, or the dancing, or the food either.

_____

3 We didn't see anything interesting.

_____

4 We won't go back, ever.

_____

4 Decide which sentences need a preposition after the verb. Put in the preposition where it is required.

1 Quiero _____ ir a un concierto.

2 Voy_____ ir el sábado.

3 Tengo _____ ir con mi hermano.

4 Prefiero _____ ir con mis amigos.

5 He decidido _____ invitar a mi novia.

6 Empezamos _____ salir hace un mes.

7 Acaba _____ terminar con mi mejor amigo.

Checklist

This chart shows the topics, skills and grammar covered in Unit 3B. Use the symbols from the key to fill in the right-hand column of the table. This will help you to see what you need to spend some more time on.

Key

☺	I know/can do this very well
☺	I'm not too sure I know/can do this
☹	I don't know/cannot do this well enough

Unit 3B Cine y televisión I can ...	How confident am I?
... describe a film.	
... express my opinion of a film or book.	
... say what I think of a star.	
... talk about an artist's career.	
... compare and evaluate styles.	
... compare what I like now with what I used to like.	
... avoid repetition in writing.	
... use a dictionary for reading.	
... break down compound words.	
... use negatives.	
... use verbs that take prepositions.	

Unit 4A Mis vacaciones

Escenario: Oral

🔊 Students' Book page 121

School trip
In Spanish schools, classes sometimes get to go on a special trip to celebrate finishing the year. Your job is to make plans for a trip your class would enjoy.

Preparing the task

1 Decide on a destination.
- This may possibly be a Spanish destination or an invented place.
- You can research places, but make sure you spend most of the time preparing your Spanish.

2 Use the Students' Book to find as many ways of talking about the future as you can.
- You can use the future tense, 'going to' or the other expressions you saw in Unit 3A.
- Look through Unit 4A and make sure you have ideas and language to cover all the parts of the task: travel, stay, food, activities, weather, justification.
- Decide who is going to cover which areas.

3 Think about ways to show off more Spanish:
- sentences with 'if',
- mention previous experience,
- use speech to say what other people think.

4 Prepare some visual support and think of ways to persuade the group that it's a good idea.
If you structure the presentation so one of you is asking the other questions, it makes it lively and easier to follow.

5 You will have to answer some questions, so think about what they might be.
Have something ready to deal with difficult or annoying questions. Maybe you could answer a question with a question!

Performing the task
Concentrate on getting your message across. If you get stuck, use your opinions and future expressions to keep talking about the activities. Use connecting words to extend and develop your ideas. Make it sound as if you are really trying to convince the group. Be prepared to be flexible and cover up any gaps when your partner has a moment.Listen carefully to questions and build an answer out of Spanish you know.

Escenario: Oral

Students' Book page 121

Dear Mum and Dad
Write a letter to parents with an overview of the trip you have planned.

Preparing the task

1 Think about the skills and grammar you will need to complete the task:

future tense	other future expressions
connecting words	time words
adjectives	comparative/superlative
opinions	verb + infinitive
imperfect/preterite/perfect/present/	

2 Match the Spanish in your toolkit to the parts of the task:
- **proposal (why you are writing, what you are planning)**: present continuous
- **transport details, activities**: future and future expressions, verb + infinitive, connecting words, time words
- **persuasion**: adjectives, comparative/superlative, intensifiers
- **refer to success of previous trips**: preterite

3 Use Unit 4A to make sure you have all the vocabulary you need and expressions suitable for writing a formal letter. Plan logical sections to your letter.
You can make five bullet points of eight words (maximum) to remind you of important points.

Writing the task

Don't get stuck with fancy starter sentences. Get on with explaining the trip. Build the letter out of Spanish you know. Use your dictionary to check words, but not to write whole sentences. Use the advice on page 7 of this book to check your work.

Gramática en acción

📎 Students' Book page 118

1 Ser or estar? Categorise these concepts correctly with ser or estar, then write a sentence as an example of each one.

> materials   nationality   temporary state   personality
> profession   time   moods   location

2 Rewrite these sentences using the future tense.

1 Voy a ir de vacaciones. _____

2 Enrique va a alojarse en un hotel. _____

3 Vamos a ir a Costa Rica. _____

4 Van a visitar la costa. _____

5 ¿Adónde vas a ir? _____

6 ¿Quién va a ir en avión? _____

7 Vais a pasarlo bomba. _____

3 Translate these sentences into Spanish.

1 We used to go on holiday to Spain, but last year we went to the Dominican Republic.

2 When we arrived, it was raining.

3 We were going to go to the beach but we decided to stay in the hotel.

4 I saw a man who was dancing in the rain.

4 Answer these questions paying attention to the time reference.

1 Cuando eras más joven, ¿ibas de vacaciones?

2 ¿Dónde pasas las vacaciones normalmente?

3 ¿Adónde fuiste de vacaciones el año pasado?

4 ¿Dónde piensas ir el año próximo?

5 ¿Adónde irías si pudieras escoger?

Checklist

This chart shows the topics, skills and grammar covered in Unit 4A. Use the symbols from the key to fill in the right-hand column of the table. This will help you to see what you need to spend some more time on.

Key

☺	I know/can do this very well
☺	I'm not too sure I know/can do this
☹	I don't know/cannot do this well enough

Unit 4A Mis vacaciones I can ...	How confident am I?
... talk about holiday destinations.	
... book holiday accommodation.	
... talk about my holidays (past).	
... talk about my dream holiday.	
... compare life in different countries.	
... use clues from context when listening.	
... work out the meaning of unfamiliar words.	
... use grammar clues to help answer questions about a text.	
... use verbs in a range of tenses.	
... use reflexive verbs in a range of tenses.	
... use *ser* and *estar* correctly.	
... use ordinal numbers.	
... use expressions of time.	

Unit 4B Nuestro mundo

Escenario: Oral

🔵 Students' Book page 137

Spanish and Latin American life
Research and present to the
class an aspect of culture in
Spain or Latin America.

Preparing the task

1 It is very important to build the presentation out of language you know, not try
to regurgitate chunks of Spanish you have found in your research.
You may find useful words and expressions, but you must fit them in with Spanish
you already know.

2 Before you do your research, make a list of the Spanish you intend to use:

description	present tense
opinions	preterite (your experience)
future expressions	perfect (they have)
time words	future tense
verb + infinitive	connecting words

3 Now when you research the topic, look for ideas that fit into what you can say:

| it is very ... | they always ... | what I love is ... | when I was in Spain ... |
| you can see that ... | | they used to ... | I would love to ... |

4 Prepare some visual support and think of ways to get your message across to
the group clearly.
  • Work out ways of expanding your answers with opinions and personal
    experience, so it's not just a list of unconnected facts. You will have to answer
    some questions, so think about what they might be.
  • Have something ready to deal with difficult or annoying questions. Maybe you
    could answer a question with a question!

Performing the task

Work out ways of expanding your answers with opinions and personal experience,
so it's not just a list of unconnected facts. You will have to answer some questions,
so think about what they might be. Have something ready to deal with difficult or
annoying questions. Maybe you could answer a question with a question!

Escenario: Escrito

Students' Book page 137

Local environmental group

Do some research about a local environmental group. Take notes about their aims and activities, how many members they have, any recent campaign successes and so on.

Preparing the task

1 Think about the skills and grammar you will need to complete the task:

future tense	other future expressions
opinions	verb + infinitive
direct speech	present/present continuous
connecting words	time words
adjectives	comparative/superlative
imperfect/preterite/perfect	

2 Match the Spanish in your toolkit to the parts of the task:
- **what the problem is**: present tense / perfect tense,
- **who they are**: present tense / adjectives,
- **their aims**: future expressions / verb with infinitive,
- **their success**: perfect / preterite,
- **compare how it used to be**: imperfect / comparative / superlative,
- **quotes**: direct speech.

3 Research the environmental group you have chosen.
- Avoid copying chunks of Spanish you have found in your research.
- You may find useful words and expressions, but you must fit them in with Spanish you already know.

4 Use Unit 4B to make sure you have all the vocabulary you need for talking about the environment.
You can make five bullet points of eight words (maximum) to remind you of important points.

Writing the task

Build the report out of Spanish you know. Use your dictionary to check words, but not to write whole sentences. Use the advice on page 7 of this book to check your work.

Gramática en acción

Students' Book page 134

1 Change these verbs into the subjunctive mood.

nadas _____   compras _____

juegas _____   vendes _____

comes _____   visitas _____

2 Now use them to translate these sentences into Spanish.

1 Don't swim in the river. _____

2 Don't play with the animals. _____

3 Don't eat in your hotel room. _____

4 Don't buy a big car. _____

5 Don't sell your cat. _____

6 Don't visit the zoo. _____

3 Match the sentence halves in the left-hand column with those in the right-hand column.

Cuando llegues al aeropuerto,
Cuando tenga veinte años,
Cuando termine mis deberes,
Cuando vaya a España,

no quiero ir a Madrid.
iré a buscarte.
tengo que ayudar a mi hermana.
voy a ir a explorar América Latina.

4 Choose the correct words.

1 Vivo en Canadá desde hace / desde hacía tres años.

2 Trabajo / Trabajaba para la organización desde hacía un año.

3 Desde hace / Desde hacía un año no tengo coche.

4 Voy al instituto en bicicleta desde hace / desde hacía un año.

5 Translate these sentences into Spanish.

1 I've eaten only yogurt for fifteen years. _____

2 I haven't listened to Gareth Gates for a long time. _____

3 I had lived without electricity for twenty-five years. _____

4 I had lived in the mountains for a year, or perhaps two? _____

6 Change the verbs in parentheses into the imperative.

1 (comer) tu yogur. _____

2 (vender) vuestros coches. _____

3 (comprar) una bicicleta para tu esposa. _____

4 (escribir) un libro sobre sus experiencias. _____

7 Complete the sentences with *ser* or *estar*.

1 El planeta _____ en peligro.

2 _____ importante no contaminar.

3 El lago _____ contaminado.

4 _____ un desastre.

5 La solución no _____ fácil.

6 El futuro _____ en nuestras manos.

Checklist

This chart shows the topics, skills and grammar covered in Unit 4B. Use the symbols from the key to fill in the right-hand column of the table. This will help you to see what you need to spend some more time on.

Key

☺	I know/can do this very well
☻	I'm not too sure I know/can do this
☹	I don't know/cannot do this well enough

Unit 4B Nuestro mundo I can ...	How confident am I?
... talk about threats to the planet.	
... talk about environmental solutions.	
... evaluate eco tourism.	
... compare lifestyles.	
... appreciate other cultures.	
... read for specific details.	
... listen and take notes.	
... focus on exam technique.	
... give instructions.	
... recognise the subjunctive mood.	
... use the subjunctive after *cuando*.	
... use *ser* and *estar* correctly.	

Unit 5A Mis estudios y mi trabajo

Escenario: Oral

🔖 Students' Book page 153

Part - time jobs at school

Work in groups of four. Your first task is to discuss what kind of paid part-time jobs the new school could offer its older students. Decide what the tasks would be, the hours of work and the pay. Brainstorm your ideas and write them down.

Preparing the task

1 Make a list of all the Spanish expressions you know. That will help you be persuasive and argue:

verb + infinitive	comparatives and superlatives
opinions	intensifiers
stalling/hesitating	sentences with 'if'

2 Think about how to bring in other tenses:

> conditional – I would ...
> imperfect – they used to ...
> perfect – I have worked ...

3 Use Unit 5A to make sure you have all the vocabulary you need to talk about jobs and education.

Plan your presentation around Spanish you know and that your audience will understand.

Think of some questions and be prepared to defend your own position.

Performing the task

Concentrate on getting your message across using Spanish you know.

Listen to the other side's arguments so you can ask intelligent questions.

A group task like this won't normally be part of your assessment, so enjoy the debate!

Escenario: Escrito

Students' Book page 153

A virtual student in a virtual school

Imagine you are a virtual student who attends the virtual school. The head teacher wants to send 10,000 emails to prospective students and parents promoting the school and recruiting new pupils. He/she has entrusted you with the task of writing the email.

Preparing the task

1 Think about the skills and grammar you will need to complete the task:

future tense	other future expressions
connecting words	time words
adjectives	comparative and superlative
opinions	verb+infinitive
imperfect/preterite/perfect/present/present continuous	

2 Match the Spanish in your toolkit to the parts of the task:

Describing the school
Adjectives
Comparative/superlative
Present continuous
Opinions

Describing the day
Present
Opinions, verb + infinitive

What it will be like
future expressions

Your experience
Perfect/preterite/imperfect

3 Use Unit 5A to make sure you have all the vocabulary you need and expressions suitable for writing a letter.
You can make five bullet points of eight words (maximum) to remind you of important points.

Writing the task

Build the letter out of Spanish you know. Use your dictionary to check words, but not to write whole sentences. Use the advice on page 7 of this book to check your work.

Gramática en acción

Students' Book page 150

1 Choose the correct adjective from the box. You can reuse some of them if you need to.

primer	buen	gran	buena	bueno	grande	primera	primero

1 Mi instituto es _____ .

2 Es un _____ instituto.

3 En el _____ año estudias inglés.

4 Es un _____ profesor.

5 Mi profesor es _____ .

6 Tengo una _____ profesora.

7 Es la _____ clase del día.

2 Underline the verbs in the preterite. Then, give the infinitive of each verb.

1 Fui a mi nuevo instituto hoy. Cuando llegué, me dijeron que tenía que ir a ver al director.

_____

2 Mi hermano volvió del instituto muy cansado. Durmió unas doce horas y después se sintió mejor.

_____

3 Match up the pairs of sentences that mean the same.

No grites.
No corras por los pasillos.
No olvides los deberes.
No vengas tarde.
No copies.

Llega a tiempo.
Haz tu proprio trabajo.
Habla sin alzar la voz.
Camina solamente.
Recuerda traer tu trabajo.

4 Translate these sentences into Spanish.

1 I decided to get up late. (levantarse) _____

2 I did my make up. (maquillarse) _____

3 I got dressed. (vestirse) _____

4 I was going out. (salir) _____

5 When I realised that it was Monday. (darse cuenta de que) _____

5 Match the sentence halves in the left-hand column with those in the right-hand column and translate them into English.

Si tuviera más tiempo
Si olvidara los deberes
Quisiera

el profesor me castigaría.
ser inteligente.
aprendería a hablar japonés.

_____

_____

_____

Checklist

This chart shows the topics, skills and grammar covered in Unit 5A. Use the symbols from the key to fill in the right-hand column of the table. This will help you to see what you need to spend some more time on.

Key

☺	I know/can do this very well
☻	I'm not too sure I know/can do this
☹	I don't know/cannot do this well enough

Unit 5A Mis estudios y my trabajo I can ...	How confident am I?
... give information about schools and colleges.	
... compare different school subjects.	
... compare schools in different countries.	
... discuss part-time jobs.	
... use a question to start off my answer.	
... predict answers in listening.	
... use the conditional.	
... use the imperfect subjunctive in certain phrases.	

Unit 5B Mi futuro

¡Soy mucho más importante que tú!

Sin mis talentos, el mundo sería un desastre.

Yo he contribuído al progreso de la humanidad.

El mundo es un lugar mejor por lo que hice yo.

Escenario: Oral

🔊 Students' Book page 169

Balloon debate
You are going to take part in a balloon debate. You are in a hot air balloon with a group of other people .The balloon is sinking. One of you must be thrown out to save the lives of others. You must justify why your character must survive.

Preparing the task

1 Each person is going to work on their own character. You should spend some time together deciding on the overall structure.
   • Is it going to be a series of speeches?
   • Will there be calm and respectful voting?
   • Is someone going to play to lose?
   • Will there be any questions?
   • Could it turn into a stage-managed argument and someone being bundled out of the balloon?
   • Decide if you need to rehearse together or just go for it!

2 Cut the task down to its most important elements.
   • You need to introduce yourself, talk about what you have done in life, and talk about the future.
   • Think about how to develop ideas or points of view. Avoid giving a list of facts.

3 When you research your character, you may find useful words and expressions, but fit them in with Spanish you already know.
   • Think about how your character could interact with other characters, maybe to demonstrate their talents or to ask them (rhetorical) questions.

Performing the task

Don't worry about forgetting your facts. Show off your Spanish! Avoid stopping and conferring in English about what happens next – go for it!

Escenario: Escrito

🔊 Students' Book page 169

Career
Research a chosen career or describe the life and career of a famous person/celebrity. Talk about childhood/family/background/studies/experiences/personality/qualities, etc.

Preparing the task

1 Don't spend too much time deciding who to research. Make a choice, and then spend your time efficiently on the task.
   You may find some useful vocabulary in your research, but plan your writing around Spanish you know.

2 Think about the skills and grammar you will need to complete the task:

future tense	other future expressions
connecting words	time words
adjectives	comparative and superlative
opinions	verb+infinitive
imperfect/preterite/perfect	

3 Match the Spanish in your toolkit to the parts of the task:

Their early life:
- imperfect,
- adjectives.

Important events:
- preterite,
- time words.

Their achievements:
- perfect,
- comparative
- superlative.

Your opinion:
- opinions,
- comparative
- superlative,
- adjectives.

How they have inspired you:
- future expressions.

You can make five bullet points of eight words (maximum) to remind you of important points.

Writing the task

Structure your work so the reader's interest is maintained through the different sections. Let your own enthusiasm shine through. Use your dictionary to check words, but not to write whole sentences. Use the advice on page 7 of this book to check your work.

Gramática en acción

Students' Book page 166

1 Complete the sentences with a preposition from the box below.

a	de	con	a	de	a	de	a	al

1 Tengo la intención _____ estudiar idiomas.

2 Voy a ir a Méjico_____ buscar trabajo.

3 _____ encontrar un trabajo, compraré un coche.

4 Tienes que aprender _____ trabajar con la gente.

5 Voy a dejar _____ estudiar cuando tenga 16 años.

6 Sueño _____ ser astronauta.

7 En mis prácticas laborales ayudé _____ construir una nave espacial.

8 Trataré _____ encontrar un trabajo en el extranjero.

9 Voy a empezar _____ trabajar el mes que viene.

2 Copy and complete the table with the first person of these verbs.

Verb	Present	Preterite	Imperfect	Perfect	Future	Conditional
jugar						
decir						
tener						
hacer						
ir						
volver						

3 Write in the correct form of the verb in parentheses. Remember to use clues such as tenses of the other verbs in the sentence/time references, etc.

1 Cuando tenía cinco años, (querer) ser secretaria como mi madre.

2 Pero hoy (ir) a seguir a mi padre.

3 He (decidir) ser famoso.

4 Ayer (ir) a una entrevista y me (decir) que volviera al día siguiente.

5 Hoy cuando (llegar), las entrevistas (terminar).

6 Ahora no (saber) qué hacer.

7 Tal vez (poder) ser secretaria.

4 One of each set of sentences needs the subjunctive. Decide which one it is, and translate it into Spanish.

1 My parents don't want me.

2 My parents don't want me to be a dentist.

3 I don't want to be a dentist.

4 I need you.

5 I need to go to university.

6 I need you to go to university.

7 When I go on holiday I go to Spain.

8 When I go to Spain I think I will go by plane.

9 When am I going to Spain?

Checklist

This chart shows the topics, skills and grammar covered in Unit 5B. Use the symbols from the key to fill in the right-hand column of the table. This will help you to see what you need to spend some more time on.

Key

☺	I know/can do this very well
☺	I'm not too sure I know/can do this
☹	I don't know/cannot do this well enough

Unit 5B Mi futuro I can ...	How confident am I?
... talk about what I want to do in the future.	
... talk about work experience.	
... explore different opportunities.	
... apply for a job.	
... think about working abroad.	
... use different styles and registers in writing.	
... think about translation skills.	
... check capital letters and accents.	
... use cognates and watch out for false friends.	
... use a wide range of tenses.	
... use the present participle.	
... recognise the subjunctive.	

OXFORD
UNIVERSITY PRESS

Great Clarendon Street, Oxford OX2 6DP

Oxford University Press is a department of the University of Oxford. It furthers the University's objective of excellence in research, scholarship, and education by publishing worldwide in

Oxford New York

Auckland Cape Town Dar es Salaam Hong Kong Karachi Kuala Lumpur Madrid Melbourne Mexico City Nairobi New Delhi Shanghai Taipei Toronto

With offices in

Argentina Austria Brazil Chile Czech Republic France Greece Guatemala Hungary Italy Japan Poland Portugal Singapore South Korea Switzerland Thailand Turkey Ukraine Vietnam

Oxford is a registered trade mark of Oxford University Press in the UK and in certain other countries

British Library Cataloguing in Publication Data

Data available

ISBN-13: 978 0 19 918702 1

10 9 8 7 6 5 4 3 2 1

Printed in Great Britain by Ashford Colour Press Ltd.

Paper used in the production of this book is a natural, recyclable product made from wood grown in sustainable forests. The manufacturing process conforms to the environmental regulations of the country of origin.

Acknowledgements

The publishers would like to thank the following for permission to reproduce photographs: 5a David L. Moore – Studio/Alamy; 35a Monkey Business Images/ Shutterstock.com; 52a Sebastien Burel/iStock.com; 61a purchased from www.bigstock.com

Illustrations by: Phillip Burrows, Moreno Chiacchiera, Gemma Hastilow, Pulsar Studio.

Cover photograph by Don Hammond/design Pics/Corbis

CD track list

1 Copyright notice

Audio tracks for Foundation Workbook

2	p. 8, ex. 1
3	p. 8, ex. 2
4	p. 8, ex. 3
5	p. 9, ex. 5
6	p. 9, ex. 6
7	p. 9, ex. 7
8	p. 10-11, ex. 1
9	p. 11, ex. 2
10	p. 12, ex. 3
11	p. 12, ex. 4
12	p. 12, ex. 5
13	p. 17, ex. 1

Audio tracks for Higher Workbook

14	p. 8, ex. 1
15	p. 8, ex. 2
16	p. 8, ex. 3
17	p. 9, ex. 5
18	p. 9, ex. 6
19	p. 9, ex. 7
20	p. 10, ex. 1
21	p. 10, ex. 2
22	p. 10, ex. 3
23	p. 11-12, ex. 4
24	p. 12, ex. 5
25	p. 18, ex. 1